Trust In the Job Search Process

Trust In the Job Seeking Process

Bypass emotional upheaval and focus on the job in hand – that of applying for jobs!

Olivia Johnson

Trust In the Job Seeking Process

CONTENTS

1.Introduction

Being unemployed or out of work can be a tough place to be, but it does not have to be!

This book has been written to help to support you while you are finding a job and to share with you and to remind you that **you can trust in the job seeking process** no matter what!

In this day and age, jobs for life are a thing of the past and most people have to be very flexible in jumping from one job to another. This means we can experience many different situations from holding a job with one company for a long time and then maybe suddenly finding ourselves having to apply for short term work using the services of a recruitment agency. This book seeks to address this type of job seeking lifestyle that we all face, where highs and lows are a common experience along the road of finding a job.

I managed to get a job at the height of a recession following these principles and thoughts and I was awarded the job despite the fact that in-house staff had also applied for the job!

It was a time of intense difficulty for me where I only had one month worth of mortgage payments in the bank and was struggling to meet my next month bills. After being out of work for about 7 months I just had to find another job or I would have lost my home as I would not have been able to keep up with the mortgage payments. So I decided to write a book with the key things I learnt that led me to getting a job just in time to meet my next month's mortgage payment but it was a very stressful time as you can imagine. In this book I wanted to share with you all I learnt and what I found to be the most important things that I did and found out that enabled me to get back into work and to pay my bills.

This book will act as a type of checklist for you to consider all the various aspects that need to be taken into account when applying for a job and trusting in the job seeking process. By being aware of the road ahead I feel it will help you to plan and gear yourself up for what to expect when searching for work and for applying for jobs, and as a result hopefully remove a lot of the stress involved in finding work.

This book has been written to help you: -

- Keep motivated while finding a job

- To acknowledge that finding a job can be difficult

- To know what to expect when finding job

- To handle any setbacks as they arise

- To know how to carry on when it feels like finding work is getting harder and harder

- To be motivated to carry on seeking for a job

- To trust in the job seeking process no matter what

    To realise you can pace yourself when finding work and enjoy yourself in between

    To have lots of hope that you will eventually find a job

    To have the knowledge of the key steps or stages in job seeking so you know what to expect

    - To prepare yourself that there are a series of hurdles to

overcome in the key stages of job seeking before you and offered that job!

- To acknowledge that finding a job can be a tough calling

- To know that finding a job is a full-time job in itself!

- To realise that asking for help is a good thing whether from a friend or a professional mentor

To look at ways to handle your money at a time of very high stress

To perform well once you have been given the job

Rather than having to learn by experience as each week rolls on, this book provides you with what to expect and plan for when seeking a job from the very beginning! It also provides you with a shortcut to know what matters and what to focus on when you are job seeking.

It may save you having to go through a lot of difficult experiences before you know what to do to be successful in the job seeking process.

We look at three main aspects of job seeking: -

- Keeping motivated when you are finding work

- Finding and keeping your job

- Handling your money whilst finding a job

2.Keeping Motivated

2.1 Keeping your spirits up

Applying for a job is a tough assignment! Finding a job is a job in itself!

This is especially true during a recession when many people will be applying for the job you want. Applicants for one job can exceed 100 plus people. The competition is not only from the point of view of the sheer number of people applying for the job you want, but also because potential employers can pick and choose who they want to interview.

Being unemployed is tough even for the best of us!

When you may not be feeling on top of the world you still have to be positive and cheerful when facing the employment process. Employers only want the positive and cheerful job applicant so the very situation you are in is quite opposite to the way in which you may feel and the way you are expected to sell and present yourself.

So, keeping your spirits up is the first thing to plan for while you are unemployed or out of work.

Remember that a potential employer would rather employ the person who is happy with life, positive and able to contribute.

You may have to dig deep to get through to the other side to employment, meanwhile it is important to keep on top of how you feel. Even people who have held very senior jobs or positions in their working life find the job seeking process a very challenging one as you need a lot of self-confidence and self-motivation to get you through, just at a time when it can be very difficult to remain upbeat and confident!

There are a number of different ways you can feel better about life when searching for a job to make sure you remain confident in yourself and feeling positive and expectant.

Keep a list of those things that keep your spirits up and put them in a diary to remind yourself to do them. If your mobile phone has an alarm or calendar use these tools to remind yourself to give yourself some enjoyable activity in between your job hunting.

These activities will differ depending upon who you are but a typical list could be: -

- Doing some exercise

- Listening to some music

- Being with friends

- Having a Lovely Meal

I personally found exercise very beneficial in dealing with the stress of being out of work. By giving out energy you gain more energy and so feel more energised to focus on getting a job and reaching your job hunting goals.

So, for example you could arrange to go for a run or jog at 9 am on a Thursday morning. Begin with a 10-minute jog and then aim to double the time jogging in a couple of months' time. You could set a target like this for each of your interests to help to keep your spirits up.

Exercise tends to lift a person's mood and people will pick up on their more upbeat manner and attitude if they are keeping themselves in shape and keeping trim. You may find the same happens to you! It may be unsaid but being fit may give you that little bit of an advantage over and above other job seekers so it may be worth considering if you don't exercise at the moment. For me it was the key to maintaining a positive mental attitude, especially when the going got very tough being out of work for a long period of time.

So, you could set yourself one day a week to do something you enjoy, and be free from the demands and expectations of job seeking. This will help you feel much more refreshed and invigorated when you search for jobs and attend interviews during the rest of the week. This will put you back in control and it will be less likely for you to feel run down because you are out of work.

You could go fishing, complete a run, visit a football match or go for a swim!

2.2 Selling Yourself

It is very important for you to understand what your employer is looking for and then to sell yourself and demonstrate what you can offer and to let your possible future employer know why you are the best person for the job. The job profile or description will outline the key aspects of the job that need fulfilling by you and you can use this as a basis for listing ways you can sell yourself and meet their needs.

The employer for example may be interested in achieving a few of the following: -

- Growing profits

- Increasing sales

- Making savings

- Excellent administration

- Improving processes or systems

- Growing their customer base

- Improving customer satisfaction

- Caring for their clients

If you can demonstrate to the employer that you have successfully achieved this in the past with your previous employers it will generate the attention and interest of any future employer, and they are much more likely to offer you their job.

Use facts and figures in your CV to quantify exactly what you have achieved in the past. For example, increasing profits by 10% in 3 years, or increasing the number of clients by 20% in 2 years.

2.3 Handling Rejection

Be realistic. Rejection will happen in many different ways whilst you are seeking a job. In fact, it can happen at any stage during the job seeking process. For example, your CV may not be accepted, you may not not be offered an interview or you may not pass the assessment stage.

If you have to apply for 100 jobs and you reach various stages of the job seeking process, but do not secure the actual job, each time you will experience a feeling of rejection and it can be very demotivating indeed.

It therefore makes sense to approach the whole process of job seeking as opportunities to gain experience even if the process does not always end in obtaining the job in the end. By looking at job seeking in this way it can result in a lot of stress being released and also enables you to have more positive energy to carry on with the job seeking expedition.

Once you have experienced a rejection you have to pick yourself up, dust yourself down and then apply yourself to finding another opportunity to find another job.

This process of rejection will happen again and again and again, until you get the actual job. It is very important you have a strategy to cope with setbacks of the job seeking journey and be prepared in advance for any rejection.

Expecting that this will happen will make you prepared for any rejection and so it will be less likely to make you feel down when the company you have applied for the job lets you know you have not been successful on that occasion with them.

2.4 Pacing Yourself

Finding a job should be treated as a job in itself.

When you are at work you naturally pace yourself, having lunch breaks and finding time off to recuperate and to recharge your batteries. Finding a job should be no different.

Some people are more naturally able to pace themselves during the job seeking process than others, but it is very important for you to pace yourself. It may take many months to get a job and you will be more effective at job hunting if you pace yourself and your job seeking activity each day, and each week, and each month.

There are five key stages in finding a job.

Each stage has to be completed accurately, efficiently, and effectively. Be prepared as it may take many months until you find that job or job opportunity you are looking for. But please remain calm.

Trust in the process of finding a job and you will be much more able to relax and take things in your stride while you are finding a job. An attitude of being more relaxed and hopeful will be communicated naturally to future employers and recruitment agencies and you will come across as not a desperate case!

Believe you will get a job at some time so long as you follow the job seeking process diligently, calmly and with full motivation. It will then just be a question of time before the opportunity you are looking for arrives! So long as you follow the process from identifying the job, to attending the interview and completing the assessment then the sausage will be produced by the sausage machine!

When you are out of work you may feel you have much less control than when you are in work. One way of dealing with this feeling of stress and discomfort is to treat it as one day at a time.

There are lots of time management books available and self-help books that can support you while you go through the job seeking process. Browse through the book shelves on the high street, or visit online book shops to see what is available. Adopt some if not all their strategies and ideas to pace yourself and to make yourself feel good.

You will get a job and it is a case of keeping on doing the right things in the job seeking process and in the right order, following the process with both accuracy and passion!

2.5 Keeping things in perspective

As the days pass on one by one whilst you are unemployed it may seem more and more difficult to dig yourself out of the mire! It is however very important to keep things in perspective and know that you will get a job if you keep following the process of finding a job.

It is important though to be flexible and remember that you may have to take several jobs in order to get your dream job, and also that you may have to take a sidestep or a step backward in order to eventually move forward. You may have to apply for a job different from your past job that needs the same skill set that you possess and this might or might not lead to a similar job that you had before. It is all about managing your expectations and not setting the bar too high. Sometimes 80% effort leads to the same successful outcome as 100% and so it is important to be realistic when job hunting.

I used the same skill set that I possess but in a number of different job roles from being a buyer to a purchasing manager through to being a data input clerk, a data quality officer, a business intelligence specialist and a contracts analyst. The same skill set was applied but just in different job roles and different job contexts. I worked in the local government, a multinational electronics company, a pharmaceutical company, and a car leasing company.

I followed the steps outlined in this book based on my experience and in one case I was selected in my job application during a recession in preference to some in-house staff that had also applied for the job!

2.6 Finding a mentor

When I was at my lowest ebb my brother suggested I contacted a recruitment specialist for some mentoring and regular support.

At first, I found it difficult to justify the cost as I was struggling to make ends meet at the time. However, I decided to give it a go and what I found was that the mentor gave me some new and fresh insights into my job seeking efforts.

I also found that it lifted off a lot of pressure and guilt of being out of work that I felt by being able to talk through how things were going with a professional recruitment consultant.

The help and support I received included the following: -

· Reviewing what type of job, I wanted to do and what skills

I had to offer

· Writing and preparing my CV

· Practice interviewing techniques

Another example I have of how a mentor role can be very helpful is when the recruitment agency I was registered with rang me once a week to find out my availability. This regular contact was so very useful for me as it kept me focused on the job seeking process and away from thinking I was "unemployed" all the time! It also guarded me against a feeling of being isolated that I felt whilst I was out of work.

2.7 Reward yourself each step of the way

We see later in this book that there are a number of key steps or stages to follow when finding a job or following the job seeking process

Remember to reward yourself after you have achieved each of these steps.

Your goals are at first not to get the job but actually just to complete each job seeking step successfully. For each job applied for you need to be prepared that you may not get right through to the end of each stage of the job application.

So, for one job they may not read your CV. For another job application they may not give you an interview. For another job you may get through to the interview stage but not be given the job!

Along the job seeking road there are many obstacles that will arise and so it is very important for you to reward yourself in small ways for each success you make. This could be as small as making yourself a coffee to enjoy after you have finished writing your CV or going for a swim after you have attended a job interview!

3.Finding and keeping your job

3.1 Trust in the job seeking process

Finding a job is quite a daunting process and it is important to understand that process and to follow it while at the same time keeping refreshed and motivated.

The job seeking process is just like a sausage machine.

If you put some good quality minced meat into the machine, with some good quality skin, and the machine is working well, then the outcome of the process of making these sausages will be some great tasting and good-looking sausages!

Make yourself a personal goal to become an expert in each of the job seeking stages.

Turn it around into a process you enjoy as you meet new people, prepare your CV and attend interviews. By preparing yourself well to go through each job seeking process then you are more likely to be successful at each one.

3.2 Keep a notebook or blog of your job seeking journey

Purchase a notebook or use an online document to record all the details, experiences and thoughts as you apply yourself to the job seeking process.

This can help as an aid when attending the Job Seekers Allowance meetings if you need to as it will provide evidence of your job seeking efforts to claim for any benefit support you may be entitled to. When you are sitting in front of someone explaining how your job search is going it can be difficult to recall all your efforts without referring to some notes.

You can record anything in your notebook but some key facts to record are: -

- Contact names and addresses of recruitment agencies

- Websites visited on a regular basis

- Jobs applied for and the dates applied

Any new information or tip bits that have been recommended to you along the way

Write all the names and addresses of recruitment agencies you are interested in along with contact names and phone numbers for quick reference.

If you are rejected at any stage of the job seeking process, make a note as to the reasons why and spend some time reflecting on what you have learnt and how you can improve for the next job seeking opportunity. By not repeating past mistakes it will make you feel better prepared and more confident putting you back in control from these same mistakes again. Mistakes are just an opportunity to reflect upon and to learn.

3.3 Keep a record of your employment and unemployment history

Often on application forms they require a history of past employment and unemployment dates.

If you have prepared this in advance it can save a lot of time, effort and frustration when you apply for jobs. All you then need to do is refer to these details each time they are requested for by a future potential employer.

You may find your tax office may be able to provide you with a list of all your past employers in case you have forgotten some of them.

3.4 Focus on what the employer needs and on what you can offer

It is easy to get lost in all the different processes that are involved in finding a job from searching for an opportunity, preparing your CV or attending an interview.

Stand aside and look at exactly what the future employer is actually asking for in the job description. Reading this with your full attention and then designing your CV around their requirements is the key to successful job searching.

Remembering by focusing on what they want and need in the job will save you making CV's that are not relevant or answering job interview questions with answers that are not appropriate to the job specification.

By always having at the forefront of your mind what it is that the company or employer needs to be done in the job it will help you to focus and to make your job application tailor made to meet their needs.

3.5 How the job application process works

The job application process can be split into a number of key activities. I have listed these down so you can make sure you are giving equal attention to each one!

Each step itself represents a hurdle to jump over and it is very important to treat each step as a separate and distinct goal in itself.

Once the first stage or goal has been achieved it is then time to move on to the next stage or next goal.

The key stages of the Job application process are: -

·   Preparing your CV

- Searching for jobs

- Applying for jobs

- Attending interviews

- Accepting the Job offer

We will now look at each one in turn.

3.6 Preparing your CV (Curriculum Vitae)

When you prepare your CV, it is vital to first read through and understand exactly what the job description is asking for and to tailor your CV in response to meeting the requirements of the employer.

There are a wide variety of different CV formats to use when preparing your CV.

However, keep it simple. The ideal length of a CV should be no more than 2 pages, but it can be stretched to three if really necessary.

The sole purpose of the CV is to get you the job interview and to let the employer quickly assess if you are suitable for the job.

The key point with a CV is that it should be able to be quickly assessed at a glance by the prospective employer whilst giving further detail at the same time if required by the employer. The use of short and definite headings and subheadings are therefore very important.

The employer will read your brief profile at the top of the CV. If they decide to know more, they will then carry on to read about your skills and competencies in the body of the CV. If these match the employers needs then the employer will carry on to read about your career history. The CV should be written with more detail being given as the reader progresses down the CV.

So, your brief profile at the top of your CV is the most important part as it draws in the attention of the employer and invites them to carry on to read some more detail of your experiences and abilities.

To speed up the job application process you can prepare a Master CV and then amend it to suit each individual job application by changing the profile section at the top of the page and leaving the rest as the same.

This gives you a lot of flexibility in applying for different types of jobs. All you need to do is to change the profile section of your CV to reflect what the employer is looking for.

When you write your CV, use shorter sentences in the paragraphs to promote speed reading by the employer, as the prospective employer will have a lot of different CVs to wade through at one time and it is important that yours is written in such a way to stand out from the crowd.

Remember also to use active words to catch the attention of the person reading your CV like I *designed* the training document or **I sold** the cars.

Also be very careful to illustrate to the potential employer how your skills and competencies match those required by the employer in the job description.

A simple yet effective CV format could use the following heading: -

- Profile

- Key Competencies

- Training and Qualifications

- Career History

- Personal Interests

Let's now talk briefly about each one!

3.6.1 Profile

The profile is a brief description of why you want the job and how you can meet the expectations and needs of the job specification. If you meet the employers' requirements then the chance of achieving the next stage of being offered an interview is greatly increased.

For example, if you are applying for a job selling a service or a product you could briefly explain your passion for selling and outline your key selling skills here. Make sure you relate your skills directly to what the job specification is asking for.

By outlining your key strengths in relation to the job specification it will attract the position most suited to you. You are more likely to enjoy your work and perform well if your strengths match up with the job that best suits your skills and abilities.

3.6.2 Key competencies

In the key competencies section, you would list your key competencies (what you are good at) and strengths using one or two lines giving examples to justify them. Examples of key competencies could be: -

· Planning and Organising

· Analysing Data and Trends

· Team Working

· Selling

Make sure every sentence you write is carefully thought through and is relevant to the job specification.

Construct your sentences so they cover the three main aspects needed of what you do, how you did it and what are the benefits to the employer by using your abilities. Here are a few examples to illustrate what is needed to be written for key competencies: -

Coordinates and facilitates (what you do) meetings smoothly and effectively (how you do it) resulting in key action points leading to lower costs and increased profits (how it will benefit the employer)

Delivers training (what you do) in a well organised manner (how it is done) both in workshop settings and on a one-to-one basis enabling the students to use the software more effectively and efficiently so staff are able to work smarter and quicker (how it will benefit the employer)

Provides excellent helpdesk support (what you do) in a clear and concise manner (How you do it) to resolve issues leading to increased customer satisfaction and therefore a greater sales volume (how it will benefit the employer)

In the career history section of the CV this approach can be used with emphasis on providing evidence from your past working and career history. You would write about the key skills and behaviours and achievements you had completed that match up with the future employer's job specification.

3.6.3 Training and Qualifications

A prospective employer will be interested in your training and qualifications.

Remember to mention any training you have received or courses passed that are relevant to the job in hand.

3.6.4 Career History

In the Career History section, you would list all your achievements to illustrate how you fulfil the future employers job requirements that appeared in the job advert or the job specification that they provided to you.

In this section you are providing evidence from your past work history of your key strengths and competencies that you mentioned in the Profile and Key Competencies section of your CV.

Here you would list each job you have completed in the past, and for each job provide the following details: -

· The name of your past employer

· Your Job Title

· The dates you worked there

· Your major achievements

3.6.5 Personal Interests

By explaining one or two of your personal interests to the employer, it provides them with some information to connect with you and to get to know you a little better during your interview!

3.7 Searching and applying for Jobs

There are a number of different avenues for finding jobs to apply for today.

I have listed the key methods I used for finding jobs which these days are mostly internet based. This list though is not exhaustive and you could add to it with avenues from your own experience as well!

· Job search engine websites

· Individual company websites

· Recruitment agency websites

- Local and Central Government websites

- National and Local Newspapers

Most of these websites offer the facility to put in job alerts for you to select the type of industry you would like to work in along with the job roles. You can set up the websites to send you emails alerting you to jobs that come onto the market that meet your job search criteria.

Remember to keep a note of each website and your login and password details which can be recorded on your job seeking notebook.

These websites are great because they help to automate the job searching process and let the job opportunities come to you via email or text alert, which can relieve a lot of job seeking stress!

Be ready though, as often an employer will not notify you that you have not been selected for an interview in response to your job application and it can be very demotivating if it is not expected. Often company websites or recruitment websites are not geared up to communicating back to you if your job application has not been taken any further and this can be quite frustrating.

It can be disheartening if you apply for jobs and you don't hear back or the jobs you apply for appear as if they are non-existent, but persevere despite these setbacks and trust in the job seeking process.

3.8 Attending an interview

First impressions count the most

People respond well to first impressions. Dress smartly and people will associate your smart dress sense with a smart person! Shake hands with good eye contact and whilst being interviewed make sure you have some good eye contact now and then with the interviewer. If you look unsure or uncertain then this will come across during the interview at a time when you need to portray confidence and calm.

It is always worthwhile preparing for interviews and to remain positive throughout the interview. Practice answering some questions with a friend or colleague.

Be ready for any unexpected questions. Questions you do not expect.

Common ones you might be asked are: -

· What are your weaknesses?

· What would you do in this situation?

· How would you deal with a difficult person?

· Where do you see yourself in 5 years' time?

3.9 Assessment Tests

Book shops stock plenty of books with exercises on logical reasoning and numeracy tests. It may be a while since you did your school level exams yet by purchasing a book and completing the exercises and tests it will get you used to completing them as you may come across them during the job interview stage.

I purchased a book on logical reasoning and numeracy and practised the test examples during a whole weekend putting myself under pressure to finish the tests in a short space of time. I then had an interview later and the employer asked me to complete a numeracy test in a short space of time. As a result of practising beforehand my results were better than all the other candidates and I was awarded the job that I applied for!

3.10 Reviewing your progress

It is very important to take some time out from the busyness of job searching and to reflect on how well you are doing and what your progress has been like over the past few weeks or months. Ask a mentor or friend to enquire how you are doing and to ensure that you are applying yourself diligently to each of the five steps of the job seeking process.

In some ways finding the job and then being offered the job is only the beginning!

You now have to fulfil or even exceed your employers' expectations when you accept the job that has been offered to you.

There is now the job of keeping the job and pleasing the employer!

There are two fundamental aspects of job performance.

·   The manner in which you complete the work

·   The level of competence in which you do the work

The manner in which you complete the work describes your general attitude to the work or job.

Successful companies value a service-oriented attitude where you are willing to serve both internal and external customers with a can do and positive service style.

The level of competence with which you carry out the job is also important.

This would have been assessed at your interview stage. Paying attention to the accuracy and timeliness of your work needs to be done in tandem with a personal service culture if your aim is to build up a strong reputation within the company or employer.

One example I have is when I organised and planned a series of meetings in my place of work to develop my "individual develop plan" (IDP) which was a type of performance assessment plan. I followed the process in a systematic and professional manner and word got back to me that my boss's boss said that I was leading the way in her team out of 15 people by embracing the company's IDPs. From this example we can see that a great reputation is developed and established just by doing a routine job well!

Work on the basis of giving what your employer wants. It may be tempting to go the extra mile and think that you are doing the right thing by working that bit harder and doing something different than what the job actually requires.

Experience taught me that the employer really is only interested in you doing the job that you were employed to do to the best of your ability and not to get distracted by doing other tasks. Remember to prioritise your efforts to focus only on the job specification that was given to you when you started to do the job as that is what they really want.

If you build up your reputation in the workplace when a new project comes up or a deadline needs to be reached you will be the one asked to help out and to support the company in reaching their goals. This will serve to build up your experience and your career in the longer term in the company.

A habit a lot of people do when they start their new job is to quickly change things to try and improve the work and perform better. Changes brought in too early without the backing and support of some good experience can backfire and not work out resulting in your reputation being damaged and it takes a long time to build back up a reputation that has taken a knock!

Once you have started your new job it is always tempting to bring in changes to make your mark. You may feel you would like to bring in some changes quickly to demonstrate your ability very quickly to justify your employer deciding to employ you. You may feel you were successful in your last job and that you need to demonstrate quickly to your employer that you are successful in your new job.

Your new job however is with different people and in a new context. What worked well in your previous job may not work well in your new job. It would be better to focus on getting your head down and learning the job well before bringing in any changes that may rock the boat and then damage your early reputation.

Another way to create a good reputation is to "walk your talk". This means just doing what you say you are going to do so that you can be relied upon and carry out what you say you are going to do! Good, reliable hard-working staff are not always easy to come by and so you can establish yourself as the "go to" person when other colleagues need advice or support in their job role.

Sometimes it is worthwhile casually asking people how they are finding the quality of your work and not to be afraid to do this. People will not generally tell you directly how they are finding your work and if you are not providing the required level of service then resentment can quickly build up towards you from your colleagues or team.

Ask a colleague what they see are your key strengths when you apply yourself to your work and you may be surprised at the great comments they have to say!

3.11 Working with Recruitment Agencies

You can view a recruitment agency in one of two ways based on whether the glass is half empty or half full.

Either you see them as extremely busy and they have no time for you or you can see them as your best ally and that they are there to help you.

It is a very competitive world and lots of people will try to get into the recruitment agencies' good books to be offered job opportunities so it is important to work hard to make sure they are on your side as in a local area they are generally limited in number.

Your objective is to build a very good rapport with just one or two agencies in particular as it is very hard to establish a personal rapport with a lot of recruitment agencies all at the same time.

If you have managed to find yourself a good reliable contact in a recruitment agency then bend over backwards to keep them happy by responding quickly and accurately to requests for things like CV's and attending job interviews at the employer.

I know from my own personal experience that most of the job opportunities given to me came from one or two recruitment agencies because the chemistry matched well between me and the recruitment agency representative.

In one case I received job offers over four years without a break because I got on very well with my agency contact. In this case my contact remembered me when job opportunities arose because I could be relied on to go for the job and respond to any other request they might have had.

If you convince them you are a great candidate for a job, they are far more likely to put you forward to the top of the pile when recommending you to different companies for employment.

As you build up a rapport with the recruitment agency it is very important to give them what they ask for both speedily and efficiently. If they ask for a revised CV then prepare it and send it to them in the next few hours.

Any request for information is an opportunity to impress.

Think of the situation from their perspective. If they know they can rely on you to respond quickly to their requests when they have a job opportunity that comes up then they will associate your professional approach with working with that company and be more likely to put you forward for consideration.

Your aim is that when a job opportunity comes up the recruitment representatives have you right at the top of their minds. Your aim is to ensure they think of you when they have been approached by an employer for a great worker.

They will also know when they submit your CV to the employer for consideration that you are an efficient and positive person as you have acted in this way consistently towards them. By providing a great service to them it will motivate them to give you the opportunities in the future over and above someone else as they know they can rely on you to perform well.

Once you have given a recruitment agency your details it is very important for you to ensure you remain on their radar. Ring them occasionally to enquire if there are any opportunities that have come up since you last spoke.

One question I asked a recruitment agency was if my CV was in a format that they found helpful to pass onto employers. They explained that a different format would be better for them to load up on their database and so I quickly changed it to suit their needs.

Sometimes I found a phone call I made to a recruitment agency led to a job opportunity being offered to me there and then as they just happened to be dealing with a job opportunity at that exact moment in time!

If you are desperate for some cash this frequent contact is very important as it can lead to an opportunity to earn some money, even if it is on a short-term contract for a few weeks just to get you by.

Keep communicating with the recruitment agency even if you feel like you are being a nuisance. Ask the agency the best method they prefer you to communicate with as some may prefer emails and others may prefer phone calls. Ask them if it is ok for you to call them once a week or every two weeks to enquire if they have any job positions that have come in. It is always very important to remain positive and upbeat when communicating with them even if you may feel down with being out of work.

If you are invited to an interview by a recruitment agency it is very important to remember that you have to not only impress the future employer but also the recruitment agency handling your application.

React quickly but professionally to any demands placed on you by the recruitment agency as they have many other people, they could offer the opportunity to have an interview with and so this makes it even more important that you remain professional and dignified when communicating with them. I found quite often they would provide very short notice to attend an interview and so it is vital not to react in a stressful way when responding to their requirements.

3.12 Accepting the job offer

This sounds obvious but when you are offered a job offer it is still very important to maintain your confidence and calmness.

The employer expects you to be excited and to convey interest when accepting the job offer. The employer has been through a long process of recruiting you and in their eyes, you are the fruit of their labour, so why not ensure their "feel good" factor is maintained because of your general manner and reaction to the job offer. This will carry you through to your first day of work.

One employer mentioned to me once that they offered a job to a person who responded by saying "Thanks, I will think about it and let you know!". The employer was not very impressed with this attitude at all, and it left them in some doubt as to whether they had made the right decision.

3.13 Excelling in your new job

Performing a job well requires dedication and passion.

Listening to what is required from your employer and responding to their feedback enables you to tweak your efforts to ensure that the work you are delivering is the best that is possible.

Responding quickly and accurately to work requests will enable you to build up a reputation as the "go to" person as your work colleagues learn that they can trust you to deliver quality work and at the right time for them.

Everyone loves a great team player and by building up a reputation for yourself that you can be trusted to interpret a person's work requirements accurately and deliver it effectively will help you to excel in your work and obtain the recognition you deserve.

3.14 Planning ahead for the next job

Be ready for new opportunities as work is transitory.

You may be promoted, kept in the same job or made redundant. But things will one day change. It is therefore important to be ready for when new opportunities arise!

Update your CV at regular intervals, say once every 6 months to record any new achievements.

Notify the Personnel Department of any new qualifications you gain. When you have completed a training course for example contact the HR (Human Resources) of the Personnel department so that they can put the details on your file. In this way if any manager reviews your qualifications in case they are looking for someone to help out in their team, then your details will be all up to date.

Keep a list of your achievements as the years roll by quite quickly at work and when applying for the next job it is often not easy to recall your past achievements over the years. So, keep a list of them that you can show to any future employer or even your current employer as part of a possible effort in securing a pay rise!

4. Handling Your Money

When you are unemployed it can be a very pressurised environment particularly if you have no money coming in other than your unemployment benefits.

To ease money pressures, you can focus on three main areas as follows: -

- Budgeting

- Reducing your expenditure and saving some money

- Increasing your income

4.1 Budgeting your money

A budget is just a list of your income and what you spend your money on each month.

The aim is to have more money coming in than going out!

4.2 Reducing Your Expenditure

A good place to start is to look at all your direct debits taken from your bank account and either reduce the amount of them by changing suppliers of the services you need, or just stop paying for them.

So, you might switch energy suppliers to secure a cheaper electricity and gas tariff, or you might cancel your gym subscription that you never use.

When I was out of work, I reviewed all my direct debit utility payments and regular outgoings. By stopping some payments or finding cheaper alternatives like household or car insurance I saved the equivalent of the whole of my monthly salary for the job I had just left! It took quite a while to do this but I found it was an excellent task to do.

4.3 Increasing your Income

There may be the opportunity to do some part time work while you are job searching or to sell some of your possessions using online auction sites.

Have a brainstorm and be creative to see how you can bring in some more money into your monthly budget. It is possible to earn some part time money doing jobs like gardening or even dog walking but be aware of its impact on the benefits you are claiming.

4.4 Financial Planning

4.4.1 Managing Salary Expectations

It is very important to be flexible in your expectations regarding the salary of a particular job.

If you have been on a certain salary and find yourself refusing lower paid jobs, this might act as a barrier to becoming fully employed again with other opportunities to consider in the future.

It may seem despondent to accept a lower paid job but it may open up other doors later on to even better opportunities than you had before. I once applied and got a job on £17,000 p.a and within 3 months was asked if I would like to be promoted and was then placed on a salary of £27,000 p.a, nearly a 60% increase almost overnight!

There tend to be lower paid jobs than higher paid jobs. So, if you apply for the lower paid jobs there is a higher probability of securing an immediate income, perhaps whilst you consider other options.

By getting back into employment it gets you back into a work routine which can build up your confidence and it is much easier finding another job from a position of being employed. You will be able to keep an eye on other vacancies that come up in the company you work for and if you build up a good reputation as a hard worker it will be easier to apply for these internal opportunities.

4.4.2 Saving for a rainy day

While you are in work it is good to realise that at some day your current job may come to an end. You can plan to be prepared for that day by setting aside a regular amount of money and putting it into a savings account to cover you if your income dries up through for example becoming out of work.

A typical amount of time to plan for is to make sure you have at least the equivalent of 6 months of your regular outgoings set aside in a separate bank account. So, if you typically spend £1000 a month on all your household bills you would aim to have set aside at least £6,000 to cover a six-month period whilst you are finding work.

With unemployment benefits you may be able to stretch the amount of time your emergency fund would cover your monthly expenses to over 6 months thereby allowing you more time to concentrate on getting back into work.

4.4.3 Considering Insurance Income Protection

When you are back in work you might like to investigate setting up an income protection insurance policy to safeguard your income if you are made redundant or become out of work. This will provide you with an income for a limited period whilst you are out of work and not earning any money. It will help to cover your monthly bills whilst you are on a separate mission to find employment and to start earning some money again.

5. Trust in the job seeking process

The key message of this book is to "Trust in The Job Seeking Process"

To trust in the princess of job seeking

In this way it depersonalised the job seeking process.

The job seeking process can be very demotivating as there are so many different stages that need to be carried out that may result in rejection and dejection!

As a recap there are five key stages of the job seeking process

1.   Preparing your CV

2.   Searching for jobs

3.   Applying for jobs

4.   Attending interviews

5.   Accepting the Job Offer

Seeking and finding a job is a job in itself!

Each of the five key stages of job finding are a goal in and of themselves

Only the next stage is possible if the stage before has been completed successfully

So, it is a case of focusing on one step at a time to then enable the next step to be faced. As an old Chinese saying goes, a journey of a thousand miles begins with a single step. In this case it is a single stage!

As you achieve and complete each successive step make sure you give yourself a reward. As you carry out each step you are gaining more and more experience to make the job seeking process easier and easier as you fine tune your skills to make the job seeking process more relevant and exact.

There is a process to follow and that is called "The Job Seeking Process"

By seeing the need to find and secure a job just as a process that can be followed and mastered it takes away the emotional charge associated with job finding.

Be clinical about it and "Trust in the process"

In that way it will help you to safeguard against feeling down and unmotivated as you experience setbacks. There will be setbacks and lots of them until that day you secure the job you are looking for, but meanwhile enjoy completing each stage.

Trust in the process and the process will look after you!

Here are three exercises for you to tap into your creative side and make a drawing on the following three pages as a sort of reflective meditation.

On each of the following three separate pages draw a picture that comes to your mind and reflect on it when you spend a few minutes thinking about: -

5.1 A Job

5.2 Employer

5.3 Your Purpose

5.1 Complete below a drawing about

A JOB

<u>5.2 Complete below a drawing about</u>

<u>THE EMPLOYER</u>

5.3 Complete below a drawing about

YOUR PURPOSE

6. Disclaimer

Please note that I don't make any guarantees about the results of the information or guidance contained in this book. In this book I share my own insights and experience to support you and help you in your job finding activities. You nevertheless need to know that your ultimate success or failure will be the result of your own efforts, your particular situation, and innumerable other circumstances beyond my knowledge and control.

Neither the publisher nor the author shall be liable for any physical, psychological, emotional, financial or commercial damages including but not limited to special, incidental, consequential or other damages.

Olivia Johnson to be identified as the author of this work has been asserted in accordance with the Copyright, Designs and Patents Act 1988

Printed in Poland
by Amazon Fulfillment
Poland Sp. z o.o., Wrocław

25862800R00027